Right On Time, Andy Capp

by

Smythe

FAWCETT GOLD MEDAL • NEW YORK

RIGHT ON TIME, ANDY CAPP

ANDY CAPP of the Daily Mirror, London

A Fawcett Gold Medal Book published by special arrangement with Field Newspaper Syndicate.

All inquiries should be addressed to Hall House, Inc., 262 Mason Street, Greenwich, Connecticut.

ISBN: 0-449-14076-8

Printed in the United States of America

10 9 8 7 6 5 4 3 2 1

MY! WE ARE LOOKIN' PLEASED
BAR
WE GOT A NICE LITTLE BONUS FROM THE BREWERY, ANDY — MIND YOU, I MUST SAY WE'VE EARNED IT
I'LL SAY WE 'AVE!
WE?
JACKIE, JACKIE, THEY ALSO SERVE WHO ONLY STAND AN' DRINK
SHADDUP!
6-14
Smythe

GRR!
GRRR!
6-16

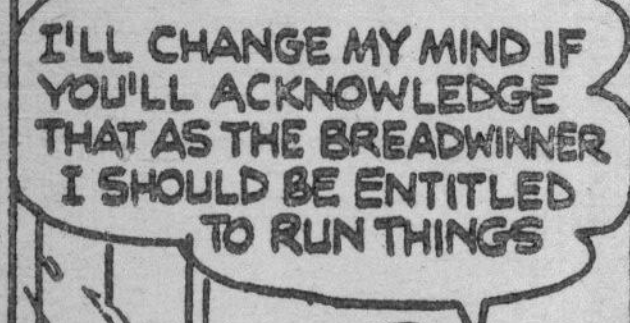
I'LL CHANGE MY MIND IF YOU'LL ACKNOWLEDGE THAT AS THE BREADWINNER I SHOULD BE ENTITLED TO RUN THINGS

AS YOU WISH. FOR A START, YOU CAN RUN DOWN TO THE BETTING SHOP
RACING
Smythe

ANDY SEEMS TO 'AVE QUITE A SPRING IN 'IS STEP, FLO — IS THERE SOMEONE ELSE?
SOMEONE ELSE—?

BAR

RUBE—THERE'S *EVERYBODY* ELSE!
6-17
Smythe

6-18

TURN THAT JUKE-BOX DOWN!
WHY SHOULD WE?

DON'T START, ANDY – YOU CAN'T REASON WITH TODAY'S KIDS

I'LL TAKE Y' WORD, JACK, I'VE NEVER TRIED – IT'S MUCH EASIER TO THUMP 'EM

6·20

'E DOESN'T ASK MUCH FROM LIFE, DOES 'E, FLO?

NOT MUCH, RUBE—

JUST A ROOF OVER 'IS 'EAD AN' ME UNDER 'IS THUMB
Smythe

ALL RIGHT! IF THAT'S 'OW YOU FEEL, DON'T 'ELP ME OUT! WHAT IS IT ABOUT ME—?
NOBODY LIKES ME!
THAT'S NONSENSE, EVERYBODY 'ASN'T MET YOU YET!
I'LL STRANGLE THAT WOMAN ONE OF THESE DAYS .... I WILL
6-21
Smythe

WE CAN'T GO ON LIKE THIS, DEAREST. I CAN'T EAT, I CAN'T SLEEP —

BELIEVE ME, PET, IT'S FOR THE BEST. WE'D BETTER BREAK IT OFF NOW, BEFORE TOO MANY PEOPLE GET 'URT
SNIFF

DON'T LOOK BACK .... I'LL NEVER FORGET YOU, BETTY

SANDRA!!
- SANDRA

KEEP YOUR COAT ON, PET, AN' WE'LL POP OUT FOR A QUICK ONE
NOT TODAY, KID, I'VE GOT NO CASH LEFT. BUT THANK HEAVENS WE'RE BANG UP TO DATE! I'VE GOT THE GROCERIES IN FOR THE WEEK, AN' I'VE GOT ALL THOSE BILLS PAID UP
YOU MEAN WE CAN'T —
SORRY
6-24
THAT'S WHAT'S WRONG WITH THE COUNTRY TODAY — BAD MANAGEMENT!
GRR-GRR!
Smythe

ANDY, I KEEP DREAMIN' THAT WE GO OUT AN' BUY ME A NEW SPRING OUTFIT — WHAT D'YER THINK IT MEANS?
A DISAPPOINTMENT — NOW WRAP UP!
6-25
WE CAN BUT TRY
Smythe

IF THERE'S NO SUCH THING AS 'A THOROUGHLY BAD LOT', WHAT SOME OF THE 'GOOD LOT' GET UP TO IS REAL FRIGHTENING!
Smythe

6-27
DUNNO 'OW THAT TWIT DOES IT, JACKIE, I REALLY DON'T!
SHOULD I ASK 'IM THE SECRET, ANDY?
I WOULDN'T LOWER MESELF!
'E'S NEVER BEEN CURIOUS ABOUT SUCCESS — IT MIGHT CONFIRM 'IS WORST SUSPICIONS THAT IT'S SOMETHIN' TO DO WITH 'ARD WORK

ANDY 'ASN'T COME BACK T' YER YET, FLO?
NO, ADA
I BET YOU MISS 'IS COMPANY, EH?
HIC
EVERY CHANCE I GET, ADA, EVERY CHANCE I GET
6-30
Smythe

SUPPOSE I'D BETTER BE GOIN', FLO, 'E'LL BE IN SHORTLY, EH?
YUP

STRANGE HAIR, FLO?
7-1

NO, RUBE, 'E'S KNOWN 'ER FOR AGES

NOTHING SERIOUS, MRS. CAPP — JUST TRY TO KEEP HIM LAID DOWN AND NO UNDUE EXERTION
MD
TRY TO KEEP 'IM LAID DOWN AND NO UNDUE EXERTION?
7-2
HEH! HEH!
HEE! HEE!
HO! HO! HO!
HEH! HEH!
HA! HA!
STAMP STAMP
WHAT A PECULIAR WOMAN!
HO! HO!
HEH! HEH!
HEE! HEE!

JUST FANCY—WE'VE BEEN MEETIN' EVERY NIGHT FOR THREE WHOLE MONTHS
THAT MUST BE QUITE A WHILE FOR YOU TO GO STEADY, EH?
7-3
YEAH, I WAS JUST THINKIN'...
CAN I 'AVE SATURDAY NIGHTS OFF?
Smythe

I THINK I'LL POP OVER AN' GET ACQUAINTED WI' THE BLOKE WHO'S JUST MOVED IN
DO, PET

MY NAME'S CAPP, MATE – COMIN' DOWN FOR A QUICK ONE?
I DON'T THINK I WILL, MISTER CAPP – ME AN' THE WIFE ARE DOIN' A JIGSAW. AN' ANYWAY, THERE'S A GOOD PLAY ON RADIO –
7-7

BLIMEY! WHAT A CHARACTER–

STILL, NOBODY'S PERFECT

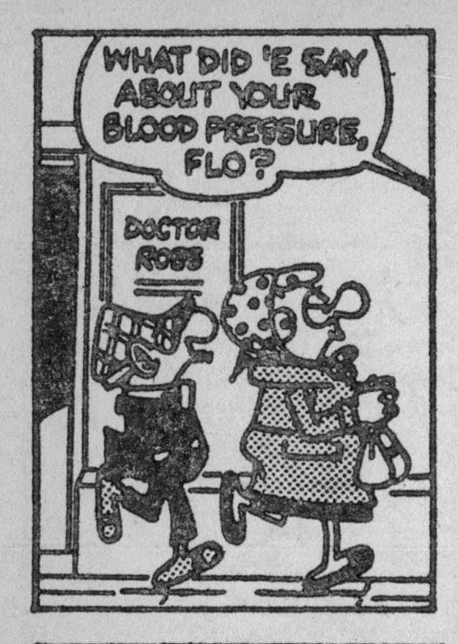
WHAT DID 'E SAY ABOUT YOUR BLOOD PRESSURE, FLO?
DOCTOR ROSS

'E SAID IT WAS NORMAL, RUBE

7-8
REALLY? OH, DEAR, DEAR!

YOU'RE RIGHT, RUBE — MARRIED TO 'IM, IT SHOULDN'T BE, SHOULD IT?
DOCTOR ROSS

GET YOUR COAT ON, PET
WHERE ARE WE GOIN'?

TOMMY GRANT SAID IT'S OKAY TO POP ROUND AN' WATCH THE CUP FINAL AT HIS PLACE — THEY'VE GOT COLOUR

BUT ME AN' ADA AREN'T SPEAKIN'!

7-9
SO MUCH THE BETTER, KID, SO MUCH THE BETTER

FEELIN' ANY BETTER THIS MORNIN', FLO?
NOPE
FEEL WELL ENOUGH TO DO THE SHOPPIN'?
NOPE
7-10
WOULD YOU LIKE ME TO DO IT?
HUH! THAT'S A GOOD 'UN—
THE PRICES'LL BE UP BEFORE 'E IS!
Smythe

GENTS TAILORING
AH-HAH! JUST THE MAN I WANT T' SEE. THAT TWO PIECE I MADE FOR YOU—

I'VE GOT A COPY OF THE BILL 'ERE — IT'S EXACTLY TWO YEARS OLD TODAY!

WELL-?

SAY SOMETHIN' — EVEN IF IT'S ONLY 'APPY BIRTHDAY'
7-11
Smythe

7-15
YOU'RE MAKIN' A BIG MISTAKE, DARLIN' —
GET LOST
I'M THE ANSWER TO A MAIDEN'S PRAYER!
NO WONDER THERE'S NOT MUCH PRAYIN' THESE DAYS

YOU SHOULD DO THIS, FLO - PUFF - LOSE A BIT OF WEIGHT...
YOU JUST GO FASTER AN' FASTER AN' STAY IN THE SAME PLACE
IT'S CALLED 'RUNNING ON THE SPOT'
7-16
I'M ALREADY DOIN' A SIMILAR SORT OF EXERCISE - IT'S CALLED 'EARNING A LIVING'!
Smythe

JUST GOIN' DOWN T' THE SHOPS, PET, WON'T BE LONG—
OKAY
MUST YOU?
BLIMEY! NOW SHE GETS UPSET IF I JUST LOOK AT OTHER WOMEN!
7-18
Smythe

I WONDER IF SHE'LL NOTICE THE LIPSTICK ON ME SCARF...?
I WONDER IF SHE'LL NOTICE IF I'M NOT WEARIN' ONE..?
TCH! THE THINGS WE WORRY ABOUT! THE FIRST THING THEY NOTICE IS WHETHER YOU NOTICE THEM
7-19
Smythe

LEN KEEPS ASKIN' ME TO NAME THE DAY. SOME-TIMES I THINK I WILL - AN' THEN I THINK I WON'T-
7-21
— I'M REAL CONFUSED, AUNT FLORRIE

WHAT WOULD YOU DO?

LET'S PUT IT THIS WAY, PET— I WOULDN'T EXCHANGE ME MARRIAGE FOR ALL THE 'APPINESS IN THE WORLD
YOU'RE NOT HELPIN', AUNT FLORRIE
Smythe

I'M OFF TO GET YOUR PRESCRIPTION MADE UP, PET
THANKS, PET, AN' THANKS FOR THE LOVELY DINNER — THAT SAUSAGE AN' MASH WAS REAL TASTY AN' THE PUDDIN' WAS GREAT —

DON'T GO ON ABOUT IT — THE FACT THAT YOU ATE IT IS PRAISE ENOUGH
7-22

YOU DIDN'T SAY ANYTHIN' ABOUT THE SOUP!
Smythe

A WOMAN'S HANDWRITIN', I SEE!

FLIPPIN' NERVE! SHE KNOWS THAT I'M A MARRIED MAN WITH COMMITMENTS!

I'LL TAKE CHARGE OF THAT—I KNOW 'OW TO DEAL WITH 'ER SORT!

THANKS, PET—IT'S FROM YOUR MOTHER, CHASIN' ME FOR THAT FIVER I OWE 'ER
7-23
Smythe

HI' YER, SANDRA
MORNIN', ANDY. I 'EAR SOMEONE PINCHED YOUR BIKE LAS'NIGHT
BAR
S'RIGHT
WHEN DID YOU NOTICE IT WAS MISSIN'?
7-24

WHEN I TRIED TO GET ON IT — HEH! HEH! HEH!

WHEN I THINK OF ALL THE LONELY WOMEN TIED TO KITCHEN SINKS WITH NO ONE TO CHAT TO, I SORT OF ENVY THEM!
Smythe

A GIN AN' TONIC AN' A PINT, PLEASE, JACK

ANDY CAPP! REMEMBER ME? WE WERE AT SCHOOL TOGETHER
QUIET WOMAN!

DID THAT LADY SAY SHE WAS AT SCHOOL WITH YOU?

ER.... YES – SHE WAS ONE OF THE BEST TEACHERS WE EVER 'AD
Smythe
7-25

I'M OFF! I NEVER GET A WORD OF PRAISE OR APPRECIATION!
7-26
SAY NOTHIN' —THAT'S YOU!
GRR! GRRR!
BUT DOESN'T 'E SAY IT WELL?
Smythe

MISSIN' 'IM ALREADY, FLO?
I GUESS SO, RUBE. I'M OFF ME FOOD AN' CAN'T SLEEP NIGHTS
IN CASE YOU'RE INTERESTED, I DIDN'T EAT OR SLEEP YESTERDAY OR THE DAY BEFORE —
URK!
AN' I DON'T CARE A DARN IF I DON'T EAT OR SLEEP TODAY OR TOMORROW, EITHER!
7-28
Smythe

7-29
FLO! F' PETE'S SAKE! STOP TOSSIN' AN' TURNIN'
SORRY, PET. DID I DISTURB YOU? I JUST CAN'T GET TO SLEEP FOR WORRYIN' ABOUT ALL THOSE BILLS

SO TRY COUNTIN' SHEEP

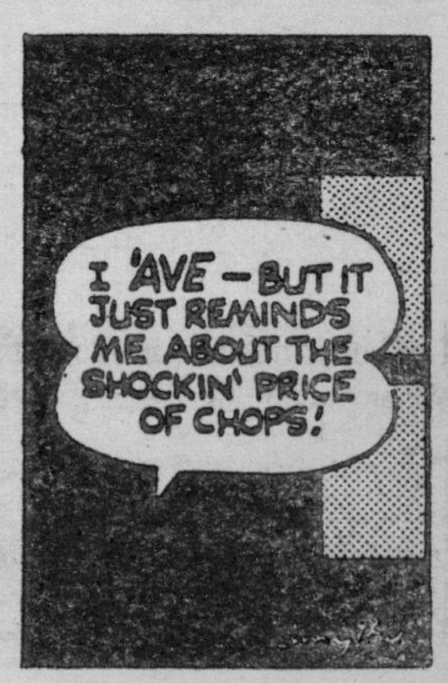
I 'AVE – BUT IT JUST REMINDS ME ABOUT THE SHOCKIN' PRICE OF CHOPS!

YOU COULD 'AVE SAVED YOUR LEGS, JACK - I HIRED A LOVELY LITTLE BARMAID F' YER WHILE YOU WERE DOWN AT THE LABOUR EXCHANGE
7-31

WHAT'S 'ER HISTORY, ANDY?

DUNNO, JACKIE, I DIDN'T GET BEYOND 'ER GEOGRAPHY!

THANKS, ANDY — SOUNDS GREAT
DON'T MENTION IT

THANKS, SWEET'EART — I'M GASPIN'
8-1
YOU DON'T KNOW 'OW TO TREAT A WIFE, THAT'S YOUR TROUBLE!
WOMEN SURE ARE A PROBLEM, EH, ANDY?
OH, I WOULDN'T SAY THAT, ERIC
I'VE ALWAYS FOUND 'EM A SOLUTION
Smythe

TCH! THE TIME! NOW FOR IT....

THEY'VE DEVELOPED THE ART OF SAYIN' NOTHIN' IN A WAY THAT LEAVES NOTHIN' UNSAID!
8-2
Smythe

HI'YER, KID
HI'YER? YOU DON'T CARE TUPPENCE FOR ME, D'YER!
DON'T BE SILLY, PET – I'D LAY DOWN AN' DIE F' YER
IF IT'S ALL THE SAME TO YOU – I'D RATHER YOU STOOD UP AN' WORKED F' ME!
8-4
MERCY ON US! WILL SHE NEVER GIVE IT A REST?

I WOULDN'T PUT UP WITH IT IF IT WAS MY 'USBAND, MRS. CAPP — YOU'VE GOT A LOT OF PATIENCE, I MUST SAY
TRIP

I'VE GOT NO MORE THAN YOU, MISSUS — I JUST MAKE THE EFFORT TO USE MINE, THAT'S ALL!
8-5

SANCTIMONIOUS TWIT

TCH! THE TIME —I SHOULD BE ASHAMED OF MESELF...

POOR FLO.... NEVER MIND, I'LL MAKE IT UP TO 'ER —

I 'EARD A LOVELY BIT OF GOSSIP IN THE PUB TONIGHT, PET
PUT THE KETTLE ON, KID, I'LL BE RIGHT DOWN!
IF IT'S A CHOICE BETWEEN A GOOD 'USBAND AND A GOOD EARFUL, THEY'LL TAKE THE EARFUL EVERY TIME
8-6
Smythe

BACK IN A MINUTE, PET

8-7
NOT BAD, EH, ANDY?
NOT BAD AT ALL, JACKIE

'E ALWAYS ASKS 'IMSELF THE QUESTION 'WOULD FLO APPROVE?' DUNNO WHY — 'E NEVER WAITS FOR AN ANSWER!
Smythe

BETTING
OFFICE
NORMALLY, I WOULDN'T STOP, BUT YOU 'AVE SUCH A REFINED WHISTLE
8-8

YOU AREN'T GOIN' TO LIKE THIS, PET —
THE LADS 'AVE ORGANIZED A TRIP TO LONDON AN' I'VE BEEN ROPED IN — IT MEANS I'LL BE AWAY FOR THREE OR FOUR DAYS
CLICK
TCH! MUST YOU?

TCH! TCH! THE TIME, ANDY! WHAT'S ME MISSUS GOIN' T' SAY--!
LISTEN, STUPID! WHY DON'T YOU SAY SOMETHIN' FOR A CHANGE? MARCH IN THERE AN' TELL 'ER WHERE T' GET OFF!
YES, ANDY -I WILL, I WILL
8-11
I WILL, I WILL...

'E WON'T, Y'KNOW -'E'LL MARCH IN THERE AN' GIVE 'ER A GOOD LISTENIN' TO

A HUSBAND CAN BE THE GREATEST BLESSIN' OR THE GREATEST CURSE OF A WOMAN'S LIFE -

8-12

BUT SHE'S NEVER QUITE DECIDED WHICH!
Smythe

MMM, VERY NICE —

I WAS JUST THINKIN', DARLIN', YOU'VE GOT THAT CERTAIN SOMETHIN' —

8-13

AN' FROM WHAT I'VE 'EARD, *YOU'VE* GOT THAT CERTAIN *NOTHIN'* — SHOVE OFF!

OOOO! THEY'RE GETTIN' 'ARD
Smythe

8-14
BANG
BANG
BANG
DON'T TELL ME, LET ME GUESS - YOU 'APPENED TO BE PASSIN' SO YOU THOUGHT YOU'D DROP IN?

I'VE COME BACK TO YOU, PET—

WAKEY, WAKEY —I COULD BE A THIEF WALKIN' IN!
8-15

I COULD BE A THIEF WALKIN' OUT, TOO —IT LOOKS LIKE IT'S ALREADY BEEN BURGLED!
Smythe

8-16
OH, NO YOU DON'T-!
STAFF ENTRANCE
I'M SICK OF THIS BATTLE EVERY FLIPPIN' PAY DAY-!
IS THERE ANY CHANCE OF YOU PAYIN' ME MONTHLY IN FUTURE?
STAFF ENTRANCE
SHE'S GOT A POINT - IT'S A BIT WEARIN' HAVIN' TO GO THROUGH THIS EVERY WEEK
Smythe

MABEL-!
FLORRIE-!
HAVEN'T SEEN YOU SINCE WE WERE IN THE GIRL GUIDES TOGETHER! THOSE WERE THE DAYS —
—WHERE ARE YOU LIVING NOW?
OH— ER—WELL, NOT FAR FROM 'ERE— A VERY FRIENDLY LITTLE STREET
A FRIENDLY LITTLE STREET —THAT'S WHERE THE HOUSES LEAN SIDEWAYS TO HOLD EACH OTHER UP
8-18

I MUST TELL YOU THIS FUNNY STORY I 'EARD AT WORK TODAY, PET—
THERE WAS THIS WOMAN WHO WENT INTO A CHEMIST'S SHOP AND—
SOME OTHER TIME, EH?
HEH! HA! HA! HA! HEH! HEH!
'E PREFERS 'IS COMEDY ON THE BOX —ESPECIALLY WHEN THEY 'AVE A SOUND TRACK TO LAUGH AT THE JOKES FOR 'IM
8-19
Smythe

THE PEOPLE YOU GET IN 'ERE, JACKIE! THIS YOUNG LADY 'APPENS TO 'AVE A B.A.
EVENIN', ALL
HI, THERE, FLO
WHAT'S SO SPECIAL ABOUT HER?
SHE 'APPENS TO 'AVE A J.O.B.
8-20
Smythe

STAFF ENTRANCE
HI, THERE, RUBE
HI, FLO—
FANCY YOU WEARIN' YOUR NEW SHOES FOR WORK! I'D 'AVE THOUGHT YOU'D KEEP THEM FOR BEST
I KNOW, PET. BUT I'M TRYIN' TO MAKE THEM LOOK OLD BEFORE ANDY REALISES THEY'RE NEW.
LIFE SURE GETS COMPLICATED, DON'T IT?
8-21
Smythe

WELL, DID SHE PASS 'ER PHYSICAL?
SHADDAP
8-23
Smythe

WHAT KEPT YOU?

THE BOSS 'AS STARTED SEARCHIN' US BEFORE WE LEAVE
OH, 'E 'AS, 'AS 'E? NOBODY INSULTS MY WIFE !

8-25

IT'S OKAY, PET. 'E SAYS IT'S NOT FOR PILFERIN' –'E JUST LIKES FRISKIN' THE LASSES
Smythe

BOOF
8-26

WHY DON'T YOU LOOK WHERE I'M GOING ?!

I THINK I MIGHT WALK THAT LITTLE DARLIN' 'OME, JACKIE

YOU'D BETTER GET IN THERE FAST, ANDY— AT LEAST A DOZEN BLOKES IN 'ERE 'AVE 'AD THE SAME THOUGHT!

NO TROUBLE, JACK, NO TROUBLE—

THAT'S ALL THEY EVER DO -THINK ABOUT IT
8-27

COR! DID YOU 'EAR THAT? MAKES YOU WANT TO PUKE – AN' JUST LOOK AT 'IM–!

PARTY POLITICAL BROADCAST?
YEAH

'E INSISTS ON LISTENIN' TO THEM–

GETS 'IS BEST REASONS FOR STAYIN' AT THE BOTTOM BY WATCHIN' THE BLOKES AT THE TOP!
PS
8-28

I'M WORRIED, CAN I TALK T' YER, PET?
NO!
'E ONLY TELLS ME 'IS TROUBLES TO STOP ME TALKIN' ABOUT MINE!
8-29
Smythe

GET A MOVE ON, ANDY - IF WE DON'T GET DOWN THERE QUICK WE WON'T GET A TABLE!
COMING, CHALKIE!
DON'T TELL ME YOU'RE GOIN'! YOU'D DO Y'SELF A JOLLY SIGHT MORE GOOD STAYIN' IN FOR A COUPLE O' NIGHTS -
'OW D'YER EXPECT TO HOLD A CUE IN THAT CONDITION?
8-30
IT TAKES MORE THAN A FRACTURED HAND TO STOP ANDY HAVIN' 'IS GAME OF SNOOKER
Smythe

THE NEW BARMAID GAVE YOU THE EYE?

SPOOKY, THAT— 'OW DID SHE KNOW?
9-1
Smythe

'AVEN'T YOU GOT A SMILE TO SPARE FOR AN OLD FLAME, PEGGY?

ANDY! MY, 'OW YOU'VE CHANGED SINCE I LAST SAW YOU!

FOR BETTER OR WORSE?
COME 'ERE AN' I'LL TELL YER —

STAY 'ERE AN' I'LL TELL YER — YOU COULD ONLY CHANGE FOR THE BETTER!
9-2

'OW'S IT GOIN', ALBERT?
OH, NOT TOO BAD, ANDY, JUST SO-SO
BAR
'OW'S IT WITH YOU?
FINE, ERIC, FINE

'E'S THE ONLY BLOKE I KNOW WHO SAYS "THESE ARE THE DAYS"
9-3
Smythe

YOU SHOULD SEE MY WAGES, PET! MIND YOU, THE OVERTIME WORK IS CRIPPLIN' ME —
'ARD WORK NEVER 'URTS ANYBODY
FINISH IT—!
—ESPECIALLY THOSE WHO NEVER DO ANY
9-4
SADIST!
Smythe

'OW ABOUT POOR FLO STANDIN' THERE ALL ON 'ER OWN, ANDY?

OH, SHE'S ALL RIGHT, SANDRA. SHE 'AD THE PLEASURE OF ME COMPANY LAS'NIGHT

'E'S RIGHT, DEAR, AN' VERY ROMANTIC IT WAS.... 'IS 'EAD WAS ON ME SHOULDER —

AN' ME MOTHER WAS CARRYIN' 'IS FEET!
9-5
Smythe

HELP!!

I DIDN'T WANT TO START ANY DISPUTES. YOU KNOW WHAT BLOKES ARE LIKE THESE DAYS IF THEY THINK YOU'RE TRYIN' TO DO THEIR JOB
9-6

DID 'E REACH A DECISION ABOUT COMIN' BACK T' YER, FLO?
RENT
NO, PERCY
RENT
MUST BE VERY LONELY FOR YOU, DARLIN' —
RENT
NOT REALLY, PERCY – 'E POPS IN QUITE A BIT TO DRINK IT OVER
GRR! GRR!
EEK!
9-8
Smythe

YOU COULDN'T FARE BETTER IF YOU WERE IN 'OSPITAL, EH, PET?
OH, I DON'T KNOW — PATIENTS GET A CHOICE OF MENU THESE DAYS
I'LL GIVE YOU A CHOICE — TAKE IT OR LEAVE IT!
9-9
Smythe

WHO'S IT TO BE — ME OR HER?
SHHH!
I'M ASKIN' YOU — I DON'T CARE IF SHE DOES HEAR!
9·10
I'VE NO SYMPATHY FOR 'ER — YOU'D THINK ANYBODY CLEVER ENOUGH TO HOOK ME WOULDN'T BE DAFT ENOUGH TO TRY AN' LAND ME!
BOP!
Smythe

WATCH IT, PET-!

WOMEN DRIVERS!

AS A MATTER OF FACT, IT WASN'T A WOMAN, PET — IT WAS A MAN
9-11

WEL-LL, 'E DRIVES LIKE A WOMAN!
Smythe

OH-OH! WATCH IT, MATE, DON'T GIVE ANYTHIN' AWAY...

9-12

THERE'S SOMETHIN' GOIN' ON 'ERE — YOU HAVEN'T EXCHANGED A SINGLE GLANCE!

GRR! GRRR!
9-15

AT LEAST I'M LEFT WITH SOME TRULY WONDERFUL MEMORIES —

LIKE THE DAYS WHEN I WAS SINGLE!
SLAM
Smythe

I'VE GOT A BIT O' TIME ON ME HANDS TONIGHT, PET— ANY SUGGESTIONS?
DO A BIT OF VISITIN'

WHO SHOULD I VISIT?
PLEASE YOURSELF

BAR
I DECIDED TO VISIT ME MONEY
9-16
Smythe

THE WAITER'S TAKEN TWO WEEKS OFF TO GET MARRIED, ANDY
SERVICE
'E'S JUST 'AD TWO WEEKS OFF — WHY DIDN'T 'E GET MARRIED THEN?
VICE
'E DIDN'T WANT TO SPOIL 'IS 'OLIDAY
9-17
FAIR ENOUGH
Smythe

9-18
DOESN'T ANYBODY EVER SPEAK IN THIS PLACE?

THE PEOPLE IN THESE PARTS NEVER SPEAK TO STRANGERS, MISS—

BUT THEY HOPE YOU DO

HUH! SOME DATE THIS IS GOIN' TO BE!
COULD YOU HELP A BIT FURTHER, PET? A POUND DOESN'T GO VERY FAR THESE DAYS—
IF YOU INSIST
9-19
I'LL COME WITH YOU. A POUND GOES A LOT FURTHER IF IT'S ACCOMPANIED BY A BIT OF SENSE, EH?
Smythe

STAFF
ENTRANCE

GET YOUR BACK INTO IT!!

9-20

MY MISTAKE WAS BUYIN' A FEW SHARES IN THE COMPANY – NOW 'E WORRIES ABOUT MY WORK-RATE!

"WE HOPE YOU HAVE ENJOYED THE BOXING, WE NOW RETURN YOU TO THE STUDIO"

THANKS FOR LENDIN' IT T' ME

9-22
ANYTHIN' ELSE?

MAY I 'AVE THIS DANCE?
Smythe

'OW WAS YOUR TRIP TO THE SEASIDE, ANDY?

RUGGED, CHALKIE, *RUGGED*—

THE ONLY PUB WAS CLOSED — SO WE 'AD TO SIT ON THE BEACH AN' LOOK AT THE SEA ALL FLIPPIN' AFTERNOON!
9-23

TCH! POOR YOU!
YEAH

JUDGIN' FROM LAS'NIGHT, 'E'LL PROBABLY 'AVE A TERRIBLE 'ANGOVER. IF YOU PUSH 'IM TOO 'ARD YOU'LL PROBABLY GET A FAT LIP...
RENT
9-24
THAT'S NOT THE WAY TO APPROACH IT, MATE – THINK POSITIVELY!
RENT
I'M POSITIVE I'LL GET A FAT LIP
Smythe

COULDN'T BEAR TO THINK OF ME ENJOYIN' LIFE ON MY OWN, EH?

IF YOU SAY SO

I'VE SUPPED AS MUCH AS I LIKED, EATEN JUST WHAT I'VE LIKED, STAYED OUT ALL NIGHT WHEN I LIKED —

AND, BOY, DID I 'AVE AN UPSET STOMACH!
9-25

I PASSED YOU ON THE BUS — WAS THAT MRS. POTTS YOU WERE TALKIN' TO?
THAT'S RIGHT—
9-26
SHE WAS DITHERIN' ON 'ER DOORSTEP, WONDERIN' WHETHER TO LEAVE 'OME —SO I MADE 'ER MIND UP FOR 'ER AN' CARRIED 'ER BAGS TO THE STATION
?
WEL-LL, 'ER 'USBAND BOUGHT ME DRINKS ALL LAS' NIGHT, AN' IT WAS THE ONLY WAY I COULD THINK OF REPAYIN' 'IM
Smythe

IT'S A SCANDAL, THE WAY YOU TREAT THAT LOVELY WIFE O' YOURS! SOMEBODY OUGHT TO TEACH YOU A LESSON!
OKAY, PAL, LET'S DO IT WHILE YOU'RE STILL IN THE MOOD —OUTSIDE!
RENT
9-27

ME AN' MY BIG MOUTH!
GRR! GRRR!

TCH

LOVELY WEATHER WE'RE HAVIN'
Smythe

LOOK, ALL I'M TRYIN TO SAY IS —
9-29
— AW, FIDDLE FADDLE!!
SHE SOUNDS REAL MAD, ANDY — 'OW DO YOU ALWAYS MANAGE TO ANNOY 'ER ?
PRACTICE, CHALKIE, PRACTICE
Smythe

WOULD YOU GIVE ANDY A SHOUT F' ME, FLO?
'E'S JUST GONE OUT, CHALKIE
WAS 'E GOIN' DOWN T' THE PUB?
I WOULDN'T THINK SO —'E WAS ONLY WALKIN'
9-30
Smythe

SNIFF
I 'EAR SHE'S LEFT 'IM FOR GOOD THIS TIME —
I'M TRYIN' T' READ
10-1

POOR BLOKE—
I'M TRYIN' T' READ

IT'S ALL RIGHT FOR YOU, BUT WHAT'S A HOME WITHOUT A WIFE?

QUIET!!

I'VE BOUGHT A LOVELY NEW COAT PET — BUT IF YOU DON'T LIKE IT I'LL CHANGE IT.
TAKE IT BACK, WE CAN'T AFFORD IT!
HELENE'S
☆@✱☆@!!
THAT'S MY OPINION OF YOU—!
—AN' IF YOU DON'T LIKE IT, I'LL CHANGE THAT, TOO
HELENE'S
10-2
Smythe

NO, MOTHER, NO LUCK WITH THE JOB — 'E FAILED THE APTITUDE TEST
HUH! IT MUST BE WONDERFUL TO BE A TWIT!
NOW LISTEN, YOU—
GET TO SLEEP —I'VE GOT NOTHIN' TO SAY
WE KNOW THAT—SO WHY KEEP POPPIN' ROUND TO PROVE IT?
10-3
Smythe

PET—
I'M READIN'!
I WONDER WHAT'S THE MATTER WI' BILLY—?
TCH! TCH! TCH—!
MARVELLOUS, ISN'T IT? 'E'LL LISTEN TO ANYBODY'S TROUBLES BUT MINE
10-4

10-6
DO YOU EVER TAKE SEPARATE 'OLIDAYS, FLO?
FISHING HOLIDAYS
RENT

YES, JACK, LAST YEAR I WENT TO BLACKPOOL WITH ANDY - AN' PERCY WENT TO WHITLEY BAY WITH 'ER
Smythe

HIRE PURCHASE
10-7
SORRY, MISSUS, WE'RE JUST DOIN' OUR JOB—
MIND DROPPIN' ME OFF AT THE ROSE AN' CROWN?
SAY WHAT YOU LIKE, YOU'VE GOT TO ADMIRE 'IS POISE
HIRE PURCHASE
Smythe

KEEP YOUR VOICE DOWN, LOVE, ME MOTHER-IN-LAW 'AS JUST WALKED IN
10-8
I DON'T KNOW WHY SHE BOTHERS YOU SO MUCH - SHE NEVER SAYS A WORD!
SO KEEP YOUR VOICE DOWN - SHE ONLY KEEPS 'ER MOUTH SHUT SO'S 'ER EARS CAN WORK TWICE AS FAST
Smythe

SHE'LL NEVER GET OUT OF THAT BED WHILE SHE'S GOT ME STUCK 'ERE PLAYIN' NURSE...
I'M OFF FOR A DRINK, PET, DUNNO 'OW LONG I'LL BE —
THERE'S FOOD IN THE PANTRY IF YOU FEEL WELL ENOUGH TO GET UP WHILE I'M OUT
'OW COULD I POSSIBLY FEEL WELL ENOUGH TO GET UP WHEN I KNOW YOU'RE OUT THERE SPENDIN' MY MONEY?
10-9 Smythe

'E'LL GIVE YOU THE COAT OFF 'IS BACK – AS LONG AS 'IS MONEY'S IN 'IS PANTS POCKET!

RENT

10-10

Smythe

YOU'LL SEE! IF NOTHIN' ELSE, YOU'LL MISS MY COMPANY!
10-11

'E'S ALWAYS MISSED MY COMPANY – 'E'S SLEPT RIGHT THROUGH IT!

I'M SICK O' THIS, MATE - PROPPIN' A BAR UP EVERY NIGHT! IF IT SUITS YOU, FAIR ENOUGH —

BUT IT DOESN'T SUIT ME! I'M FINISHED —GOODBYE!

SUIT Y'SELF, KIDDO

IF ME MISSUS ASKS ME WHAT I SAW IN YOU — WHAT SHOULD I TELL 'ER?!
Smythe
10-13

10-14
HEH! HEH! CHEEKY!
FAMILY BUTCHER

I LIKE THAT BLOKE. ALWAYS MANAGES T' SAY SOMETHIN' NICE T' YER – IS ANDY ONE FOR COMPLIMENTS?

WELL, 'E DID ONCE SAY WHAT LOVELY HANDS I HAD –

WE WERE PLAYIN' POKER AT THE TIME!
Smythe

REMINDS ME OF THE NIGHT 'E PROPOSED TO ME WITH BENDED KNEE, FLO
10-15
BAR

I'M REMINDED ALL THE TIME, MARTHA —'E DID IT WITH BENDED ELBOW
Smythe

TEA'S ON THE TABLE, PET, COME AN' GET IT
10-16
— TEA'S READY

I SAID TEA'S READY!!
Smythe

HANG ON, FLO —LET ME HELP YOU!
DEFINITION OF A GENTLEMAN IN THESE PARTS — A BLOKE WHO HOLDS THE DOOR OPEN WHILE THE PACK-HORSE CARTS THE STUFF IN
10-17
Smythe

ANDY'S IN THE OTHER ROOM, FLO
I BOUGHT 'IM A DRINK AND 'E BOUGHT ME ONE BACK
SO-?
WOULD YOU TAKE THESE ORDERS WITH YOU-
?
'E RETURNED THE DRINK BUT KEPT THE WAITRESS
10-18

THEY'RE CELEBRATIN' —OBSERVIN' SOME SORT OF ANNIVERSARY

10-20

'E DOES THE CELEBRATIN' —SHE DOES THE OBSERVIN'!
Smythe

TRAVEL AG
EXCURSIONS
EVENING MYSTERY TOURS
WHY DON'T WE ALL GO ON ONE OF THESE MYSTERY TOURS, FLO? IT MIGHT BE A BIT O' FUN!
DON'T YOU BELIEVE IT, RUBE —
10·21
'IM AN' ME WENT ON ONE LAST YEAR AN' WE STOPPED AT SIX DIFFERENT PUBS IN TWO HOURS —
WHERE'S THE MYSTERY IN THAT?
I SEE WHAT YOU MEAN, FLO — WE MIGHT AS WELL GO DOWN T' THE ROSE AN' CROWN AN' BE DONE WITH IT
Smythe

10·22
MMM...!
KLUNK
MEBBE IT'S NATURE'S WAY OF TELLIN' ME TO SLOW DOWN

BE A GOOD BOY, NOW
AW, SHADDUP!
SHE GETS MORE LIKE A MOTHER T' ME—!
AN' 'E GETS MORE LIKE A SON T' ME —UNAPPRECIATIVE, SURLY, SPOILED, AN' CHEEKY WITH IT
10-23
Smythe

WOULD YOU CARE TO 'AVE SUPPER WI' ME TONIGHT, PET? I'D LIKE TO DISCUSS A RECONCILIATION
10·24
I'D BE DELIGHTED!
THAT'S MY GIRL—
I'LL BE BACK AT CLOSIN' TIME — YOU'LL 'AVE SOME FISH AN' CHIPS WAITIN', EH?
Smythe

10·25

COMMONLY KNOWN AS THE GENERATION GAPE

10-27
I HEAR MRS. THOMPSON'S THROWN 'ER LODGER OUT. WASN'T PAYIN' 'IS RENT, APPARENTLY
TCH! TCH! I'M NOT SURPRISED. THE MONEY 'E SPENDS ON WOMEN—

I'VE GOT NO SYMPATHY FOR A MAN WHO'S OUT WITH A DIFFERENT GIRL EVERY NIGHT

A BLOKE WHO'S OUT WITH A DIFFERENT GIRL EVERY NIGHT NEEDS SYMPATHY?

I 'AD A TWO HOUR TALK WITH MY BOSS ABOUT CAPP THIS MORNIN' AN' I FEEL SO MUCH BETTER—

— WE'VE SET UP A CALCULATED, COMPREHENSIVE PLAN O' CAMPAIGN DESIGNED T' REACH A CERTAIN GOAL DURIN' THE NEXT TWO YEARS —
LIKE GETTIN' 'IM TO OPEN THE DOOR
BANG! BANG!
BANG!
BANG!
10-28

I'LL CALL INTO MUM'S ON THE WAY 'OME — JUST TO SEE 'OW SHE IS...
STAFF ENTRANCE

10-29
I. JUST POPPED IN TO SEE MY MOTHER, PET-
YEAH, I GUESSED AS MUCH! AN' 'ERE'S ME WAITIN' F' ME TEA—!

I'M SICK OF PLAYIN' SECOND FIDDLE!

SECOND FIDDLE? LISTEN, PAL. YOU'RE LUCKY TO BE IN THE BAND AT ALL!!

I DON'T CARE WHAT YOU SAY, I'M GOIN' TO GET A NEW CARPET! I'M THE ONE WHO'LL 'AVE TO PAY FOR IT!
SUPPOSE I'D BETTER TAKE AN INTEREST...
10-30
THIS ONE IS BEGINNIN' TO LOOK A BIT TATTY, PET — WHAT COLOUR 'AD YOU IN MIND?

I THINK A SORT OF ASH GREY WOULD BE THE MOST SUITABLE!

SLAM
EVEN WHEN YOU AGREE WITH 'ER SHE GETS UPTIGHT

YOU'RE EARLY —WHAT'S WRONG?
NOTHIN'S WRONG. IT JUST 'APPENED THAT I — NO, SKIP IT — YOU WOULDN'T BELIEVE IT
OF COURSE, I WOULD
YOU WOULDN'T
I WOULD
NO, PET, YOU JUST WOULDN'T
I'M TELLIN' YOU —I'D BELIEVE IT!
WELL, I WAS IN THIS CROWDED PUB AN' SUDDENLY I FELT LONELY WITHOUT YOU—
I DON'T BELIEVE IT
10-31
Smythe

YOUR DAUGHTER'S THROWN ME OUT -I'VE GOT NO PLACE TO GO!

TCH! TCH! IN THIS STORM-!

GET Y'SELF BACK THERE AN' TELL 'ER TO BE A BIT MORE TOLERANT
SLAM

FLIPPIN' HYPOCRITE! 'ER IDEA OF TOLERANCE IS NOT MINDIN' WHETHER I'M STRUCK BY A FLIPPIN' THUNDERBOLT!

CAN I WALK YOU 'OME, BEAUTIFUL?
IF YOU LIKE
11-3
'ANG ON TILL I RETURN THIS EMPTY GLASS—
I HATE YOU!

EMPLOYMENT
I'D TAKE IT LIKE A SHOT — IF IT WASN'T FOR MY RHEUMATISM

IT'S A GOLDEN OPPORTUNITY LOST, Y'KNOW!

POPPYCOCK! NO OPPORTUNITY'S EVER LOST — SOME OTHER TWIT ALWAYS TAKES IT
11-4
Smythe

POLICE
LOCK ME UP, SARGE – I'VE JUST HIT CAPP OVER THE HEAD WITH A BOTTLE!
RENT

POLICE
IS THE POOR BLOKE UNCONSCIOUS?
POLICE
NO, 'E ISN'T! – WHY D'YER THINK I WANT T' BE LOCKED UP?
Smythe 11-5

TCH! I DON'T KNOW 'OW I'M GOIN' TO FACE THE RENTMAN THIS MORNIN' —
NO POINT IN CROSSIN' Y' BRIDGES BEFORE Y' COME TO 'EM
11-6
AND THE BUTCHER WANTS 'IS MONEY TOMORROW —
RELAX, WOMAN — TODAY'S THE TOMORROW YOU WORRIED ABOUT YESTERDAY
EEEK! THE TIME —!
'E CAN PHILOSOPHIZE ABOUT EVERYTHIN' EXCEPT BEING A MINUTE LATE FOR OPENIN' TIME
Smythe

GRR!
GRR!
YOU SHOULD GET A DOG, FLO— MARVELLOUS EXERCISE
WE'VE GOT A BIKE, BRENDA
DO YOU USE IT MUCH?
I 'AVE TO MOVE THE FLIPPIN' THING OUT OF MY WAY EVERY TIME I TRY TO GET DOWN THE HALLWAY!
11-7
Smythe

I WON'T BE ABLE TO SEE YOU ANY MORE, ANDY – MY GEORGE IS COMIN' OFF THE NIGHT SHIFT AN' GOIN' BACK ON DAYS
OH, NO!
11-8
THE BEST WAY T' GET OVER A PASSIN' FANCY IS TO FIND SOMETHIN' FANCIER
Smythe

LET ME FILL YOUR GLASS, PET
SIGH
11-10
I'M MAKIN' 'IM SO 'APPY AT 'OME THAT 'E'S BEGINNIN' TO PREFER 'IS COMFORT TO ANYTHIN' ELSE ON EARTH—
ME INCLUDED

YOU SOUND 'APPY —GOT A DATE?
I'M ALWAYS 'APPY
TAKE ME FOR A DRINK AN' MAKE ME 'APPY

BOOZE DOESN'T BRING TRUE 'APPINESS, FLORRIE—

THAT'S OKAY —I'M EASILY FOOLED

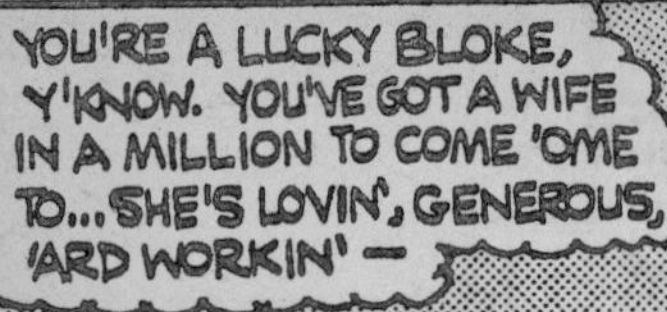
YOU'RE A LUCKY BLOKE, Y'KNOW. YOU'VE GOT A WIFE IN A MILLION TO COME 'OME TO... SHE'S LOVIN', GENEROUS, 'ARD WORKIN' —

CARIN' FOR YOUR EVERY NEED. SO TELL 'ER FOR ONCE IN YOUR LIFE — WOMEN NEED REASSURIN', RIGHT?

FLO—
YES?

YOU COULD BE WORSE
?
Smythe
11-12

HEY! YOU TWO! 'OW ABOUT A BIT LESS OF THE LOVEY-DOVEY AN' DOIN' A BIT MORE SERVIN'?
BANG
BANG

TCH! THAT FLIPPIN' BARMAID AN' THAT WAITER-!

THE SERVICE 'AS GONE TO POT SINCE THEY PATCHED UP THAT QUARREL OF THEIRS!

IT'S ONLY TEMPORARY — THEY'RE GETTIN' MARRIED NEXT WEEK
THANK 'EAVENS F' THAT
11-13

BETTING OFFICE
11-14

LIFE'S SURE BEEN GOOD TO ME....

I SHOULD SHARE MY GOOD FORTUNE... I KNOW, I'LL SPEND A BIT OF IT ON SOME LONELY OLD PERSON...!

NINETEEN IS OLD FOR A TEENAGER
Smythe

SORRY I'M LATE 'OME, PET—I GOT INTO A FLIPPIN' CARD GAME
THEY'RE STILL AT IT! I 'AD A 'ARD TIME GETTIN' AWAY, BUT YOU KNOW ME, KID — I'D GO THROUGH 'ELL AN' HIGH WATER TO GET BACK T' YER
11-15
WHAT KEPT YOU ALL NIGHT THEN?
'AVE YOU SEEN THE 'OLE IN ME SHOE? IT WAS POURIN' DOWN!
Smythe

EMPLOYMENT EXCHANGE
CAN'T TAKE IT BECAUSE OF YOUR WAR WOUND? WHAT WAR WOUND?
I NEVER TALK ABOUT IT

'E DROPPED A CASE OF CORNED BEEF ON 'IS FOOT —
11-17

MIND YOU, IT WAS IN TOBRUK —

AN' THERE WAS A WAR ON —
YOU'RE ASKIN' FOR IT —!

I SUPPOSE 'E'S OFF TO MEET 'ER —
11·18

NOT ANY MORE, RUBE. I TOLD 'IM 'OW MUCH SHE WAS SPENDIN' ON 'ER HAIR EVERY WEEK — WHICH SHE COULD'VE BEEN SPENDIN' ON BOOZE
GOOD F' YOU, FLO

NOT REALLY, RUBE — NOW 'E'S DATIN' 'ER HAIRDRESSER!